Original title:
Magnolia Magic

Copyright © 2025 Creative Arts Management OÜ
All rights reserved.

Author: Alec Donovan
ISBN HARDBACK: 978-1-80566-676-9
ISBN PAPERBACK: 978-1-80566-961-6

## Echoes through Petal-Laden Streets

Petals flurry in the breeze,
A cat in a hat climbs up the trees.
Squirrels compete in a race so grand,
While the pigeons shake their heads and stand.

Laughter dances down this street,
As old Mrs. Dobbles taps her feet.
She shimmies through, with her poodle in tow,
Singing a tune only they seem to know.

## The Dance of the Silk Treetops

Up above, the branches sway,
As if they're planning mischief today.
A squirrel steals popcorn from a snack,
While the blue jays laugh and plot their attack.

Down below, children prance in glee,
Covered in petals as sweet as can be.
They giggle and twirl, in swirling delight,
Wishing the sky could twinkle at night.

## **Lullabies Among the Blossoms**

Bumblebees buzzing a sleepy tune,
While kittens dream under the bright afternoon.
A raccoon tiptoes with a curious look,
As if searching for treasures in a storybook.

The trees sigh softly, wings all a-flutter,
As paper boats float on puddles of butter.
A frog serenades under a blanket of stars,
While fireflies wink to the rhythm of bars.

## The Scent of History's Embrace

Whispers linger in the fragrant air,
As tales of mischief bounce everywhere.
Old statues crack jokes in between the vines,
While worms in the soil share sipping of wines.

History winks with a playful grin,
As ants march in line, they surely can spin.
A tumble of petals, a giggle or two,
Prepare for a party—yes, that's what we do!

## Tales Written in Bloom and Moonlight

In the garden where flowers grow,
The rabbits dance, don't you know?
They twirl and spin in elegant flair,
Wearing top hats without a care.

Bumblebees hum a sweet old tune,
While the raccoons hold a grand raccoon.
With pickles and jam in delightful stacks,
They toast to the night, with no lack of snacks.

Amidst the petals, a mouse takes a seat,
Claiming the throne—what a funny feat!
He grins as he feasts on chocolate cake,
Squeaking his joy—oh, make no mistake!

Stars peek down with a curious glance,
As the flowers sway, they join in the dance.
In bloom and moonlight, oh what a show,
With laughter and joy that just seems to grow!

## Whispers of the Garden at Dusk

In twilight's embrace, the garden sighs,
As gnomes tell tales 'neath starlit skies.
They trade corny jokes, so silly yet bright,
While crickets croon songs to the firefly light.

A cat in the bushes spies on the fun,
With dreams of the fish he'll catch on the run.
He ponders the garden's next grand feast,
Imagining mice—as tasty as least!

The flowers snicker in soft, breezy tones,
Watching the garden's whimsical clones.
Each petal a giggle, each stem a delight,
As laughter explodes into the crisp night.

So come take a stroll, meet the quirky throng,
In laughs and in blooms, where we all belong.
Here in this garden of tales and of dreams,
Life's a delightful, wacky, wild theme!

## Embrace of the Southern Breeze

In the garden where the flowers sway,
The southern breeze has come to play.
It tickles noses, makes us sneeze,
And dances with the nearby trees.

With laughter loud, we twirl and spin,
As bees rumor tales of sweet chagrin.
A picnic blanket, oh so wide,
Turns into a bouncy, giggling ride.

But watch your sandwich, don't let it fly,
The breeze has plans to say goodbye!
Chasing crumbs that drift and roll,
It's part of the wind's hilarious goal.

## Evening's Silent Serenade

As twilight dims the summer light,
Crickets begin their concert tonight.
They chirp a tune that's sure to delight,
While frogs audition for Broadway's spotlight.

Fireflies join the glowing show,
With winks and twirls, they'll steal the glow.
But watch your drink, it might take flight,
A curious bug could end the night!

With laughs we share the buzzing cheer,
A chance embrace with the twilight near.
In this soft hum of nature's prank,
We toast to owls who no one thanked.

## Secrets in the Garden's Shade

In the shade where secrets lay,
The garden critters plot their play.
A rabbit whispers to a snail,
About the day they'll hit the trail.

But wait! A squirrel jumps in glee,
Proclaiming he must climb a tree.
He trips on acorns, makes a fuss,
The whole brigade begins to rush.

They laugh and giggle, tails in the air,
As shadows dance without a care.
The sun peeks in, a teasing ray,
To steal their fun and join the fray.

## Statuesque Beauty in Bloom

In a corner stands a statue fair,
She's watched the garden with her stare.
But gotta say, she's quite the prude,
Refusing laughter, slightly rude!

We dress her up with hats so tight,
And hang a sign, 'Join in the fight!'
Balloons and ribbons fill her space,
She blushes bright as we laugh with grace.

Yet at dusk, when shadows close,
She cracks a smile, a secret knows.
Maybe beauty's more than just the gloom,
Especially when you're in full bloom.

## Charm of the Blossoming Night

In the garden where laughter blooms,
Silly whispers fill the rooms.
Petals dance like a jolly clown,
Wearing their floral, leafy crown.

Under stars with a twinkling grin,
Frogs croak tunes; let the fun begin!
Bumblebees join with a cheerful buzz,
Creating a fuss, oh what a buzz!

Laughter echoes under the moon,
Rabbits hop around, in a merry tune.
Magic blooms in a comical sight,
As critters celebrate the blossoming night.

## Where Blossom Meets the Breeze

In the breeze, a tickle so sweet,
Flowers giggle beneath our feet.
Gathering whispers, a playful tease,
Joy floats softly on the warm breeze.

With petals winking at the sun,
A dance party just for fun!
Squirrels in bowties, oh what a sight,
Party hats worn just right!

Daisies prance with a cheeky flair,
While butterflies twirl in the air.
Laughing buds in a playful tease,
Where giggles grow, and worries freeze.

## Sweet Fragrance of the Dawn

Morning blooms with a lovely snack,
Honeydew drops spill with a smack.
Jellybeans grow from grass so tall,
While tree trunks giggle and start to sprawl.

The scent of pancakes fills the sky,
Even the slugs give a happy sigh.
Sunbeams wink with a golden light,
As the world wakes, oh what a sight!

Laughter spills like morning dew,
Silly squirrels in a joyful queue.
With each petal glow, our hearts are drawn,
To the sweet fragrance of the dawn.

## Lullabies in the Garden of Light

Crickets sing their bedtime song,
While flowers sway and hum along.
With every bloom, a tale they weave,
Of all the fun that they believe.

Moonlight paints the garden bright,
As daisies gossip throughout the night.
Fireflies dance with a sparkling cheer,
Painting wishes in the atmosphere.

Giggling buds share secrets near,
Wishing that laughter's always here.
In dreams, they twirl in a playful flight,
Singing lullabies in the garden of light.

## A Haiku for the Gilded Evening

Evening skies chuckle,
Petals dance with a wink,
Nature's laughter glows.

Buzzing bees at play,
Chasing blooms through the warm air,
Who knew they could jig!

Fireflies in a line,
Judging dances of the night,
A glowworm just sighed.

Whispers from the breeze,
Tickle leaves in silly ways,
A giggle from trees.

## Whispers of the Southern Bloom

Southern blooms gossip,
In a secret, flowery chat,
Bees hear the juicy tales.

Frogs wear funny hats,
Croaking out their loud opinions,
While birds snicker near.

Swaying in soft light,
Flowers tease the buzzing crowd,
Nature's comedy.

The sky holds its breath,
As petals huddle and laugh,
What a show tonight!

## Enchanted Petals in Twilight

Twilight has its tricks,
Petals giggle in the shade,
Starlight blinks with glee.

Crickets take the stage,
With their legs they play the tune,
A nocturnal show.

Giggling shadows sneak,
Poking fun at sleepy trees,
The night rolls with laughs.

And as the moon glows,
Each flower joins in the fun,
A whimsical ball.

## Beneath the Canopy of Stars

Stars are laughing bright,
Beneath them blooms have a ball,
Nature's party time.

Dancing through the night,
Wind whispers jokes to the leaves,
They all sway and sway.

With laughter so light,
Buds pop in the moon's glint,
Each chuckle takes wing.

Underneath the fun,
Frogs jive and crickets keep beat,
What a wild night!

## The Radiance of Petaled Dreams

In a garden where petals sway,
A chubby bee forgot his way.
He danced on blooms, oh what a sight,
Buzzing tunes that brought delight.

With tiny shoes, he spun around,
While clumsy ants fell to the ground.
The flowers laughed, their colors bright,
As he proclaimed it was a night!

## Nature's Whispers on Floral Wings

A butterfly in polka dots,
With stylish flair and fancy thoughts.
He twirled through daisies, what a show,
While snails cheered on, in a row.

The wind chimed in with gentle hums,
Tickling petals, making drums.
A rainbow formed, as colors play,
In this floral dance, no gray.

## Soft Radiance of the Flowering Night

Under starlight, flowers scheme,
They plan their pranks, a wild dream.
A rose called out, with teasing grin,
'Let's have a laugh, let fun begin!'

The daisies giggled, oh so bright,
As shadows danced in the moonlight.
Petals fell like confetti rain,
While crickets played their sweet refrain.

## Enchanted Blooms Amidst the Pines

In a forest where blooms are found,
A mischievous vine wrapped around.
It tied up squirrels, twirled with glee,
'Join our party, come dance with me!'

The pines swayed in rhythmic trance,
As flowers made the critters prance.
Laughter echoed, pure and free,
In a wild, whimsical jubilee.

## Wandering Through Blossom-Laden Dreams

In a garden where flowers conspire,
Bees wear tuxedos, and ants are fire.
Petals giggle, tickling the breeze,
As squirrels debate who planted the trees.

Butterflies dance in their Sunday best,
While frogs hold a party, they're truly obsessed.
In this whimsical world, joys interlace,
Every bloom's just a comical face.

## The Allure of Nature's Caress

Sunshine sprawls like a lazy cat,
While daisies pretend to wear a hat.
Laughter drips from the honeyed dew,
Nature's friends share jokes that are new.

Trees whisper secrets, oh what a tale,
While worms in top hats dance without fail.
Shadows stretch, yawning on the grass,
Even the daisies join in, alas!

## Blooming Souls Beneath the Stars

Stars play hide and seek with the night,
While crickets argue who can sing right.
Moonbeams giggle, shining with glee,
As blossoms compete for a starry marquee.

Night critters throw a ball, just for kicks,
Snails bring the chips; it's the latest fix.
With zest and zing under twinkling skies,
Even the shadows can't help but rise.

## Kissed by the Essence of Spring

Springtime arrives with a playful wink,
As flowers spill secrets in colors they drink.
Frogs fashion crowns, feeling quite regal,
While petals plot mischief with a gleeful giggle.

Breezes whistle tunes, oh what a sound,
As blossoms perform, twirling around.
Nature's grand circus puts on a show,
Joyful and funny as laughter will flow.

## **Blooming Under a Celestial Spell**

In the garden where gnomes play,
Flowers giggle in bright array.
Bees don tiny hats with flair,
Buzzing tunes fill the sunny air.

Under a moon that's quite absurd,
Cats give flowers the strangest word.
Squirrels hold a dance-off near,
With buds clapping, it's quite clear.

A dog tries to join the fun,
Wagging tail, he thinks he's won.
But the blooms trip him with a laugh,
Falling down, he takes a bath!

So if you wish to join this spree,
Grab a hat, it's gnome decree.
In the magic of the night,
Everything's silly, and just right!

## The Allure of Velvet Petals

In a world where petals wink,
Flowers plot and often think.
They whisper secrets on the breeze,
Tickling noses just to tease.

A butterfly, in dreams so grand,
Chased his shadow through the land.
But the petals pulled a prank,
He landed in a giggling tank!

Snails with shades and funky hats,
Dance in circles like acrobats.
The sun bursts out, no need to hide,
As blooms rejoice in flowered pride.

So laugh along with petals bright,
For gardening's a comical sight.
With every bloom, there's joy anew,
It's a party just for you!

## Shadows Dance in Fragrant Breezes

In the twilight, shadows sway,
Dancing blooms in a wild fray.
Crickets chirp a rhythmic beat,
As petals waltz on little feet.

A raccoon dons a masquerade,
Stealing snacks, quite unafraid.
But flowers giggle on the ground,
When he trips and rolls around!

Fireflies twinkle like spaced-out stars,
Flowers giggle, look at their cars!
Tiny leaves with GPS,
Drive in circles, what a mess!

So join the fun, don't be shy,
When the blossoms laugh and cry.
In the breeze, their scents will play,
Turning night into a bright ballet!

## **Echoes of the Blossom Moon**

Beneath a moon that's cake-like round,
Whispers in the garden sound.
Petals pose in the glow so bright,
Holding court till late at night.

A frog tries to croak a tune,
But blooms hum louder in their swoon.
Critters join with funny cheers,
As flowers giggle through the years.

Ladybugs sport polka dots,
Dancing in spectacular knots.
They call the ants to join the show,
What a spectacle to bestow!

So prance along in moonlit glee,
With blossoms singing, wild and free.
In this realm, the laughter blooms,
Echoing joy through garden rooms!

## **Floral Fantasies in the Gentle Breeze**

In a garden where flowers sway,
Bumblebees dance, come what may.
Petals wink in the sunlight's gleam,
While ants hold a tiny ice cream dream.

Butterflies laugh at their own clumsiness,
Tiptoeing on blooms, pure foolishness.
They chase their shadows, what a sight,
Turning afternoon into a delight.

Squirrels throw parties in the trees,
Making snacks from petals, if you please.
The scent of mischief fills the air,
Nature's joke caught unaware.

Here in this paradise, so grand,
You'll see kites tangled, by a hand.
With every gust that comes around,
Fleeting giggles echo the sound.

# Touched by Petals of Enchantment

Petals whisper secrets in the night,
A flower tried to start a kite fight.
With roots in the soil, they take a chance,
Dropping seeds and throwing a dance.

Frogs in tuxedos croak with glee,
As flowers debate who's the tallest tree.
A rose put on glasses, thought it could see,
Yet stumbled over a bumblebee.

Giggling daisies tease the sun,
Wagering who will have more fun.
With a flick of their petals, they all agree,
Every party's best when you're carefree.

Every hour, a surprise to behold,
Nature's tapestry, colorful and bold.
A petal parade down the garden path,
It's all a laughter, a floral math!

# Mesmerized by Blooming Whispers

In a meadow, the flowers sing low,
Poppy thinks it's time for a show.
Daisies twirl in a graceful craze,
While tulips giggle, lost in a haze.

A sneaky vine starts pulling a prank,
On a lazy bee that forgot to tank.
A daffodil shimmies with such flair,
When the breeze pokes at its golden hair.

Sunsets painted with pink and orange hue,
Bumblebees sporting a hat or two.
Flora and fauna share in the jest,
While the earth spins, we're all just guests.

Jasmine sways like it's part of a band,
Cattails joining in, hand in hand.
All through the garden, a whimsical ride,
With flowers like friends, joy amplified.

## Starlit Paths of Floral Delight

Under stars, the blooms take flight,
Dandelions twinkle, such a sight.
Wishing on petals that scatter and spin,
While grasshoppers laugh, let the fun begin.

A night-blooming flower put on a mask,
Hosting a party, oh what a task!
With each petal illuminated with charm,
The laughter of critters keeps spirits warm.

Glowworms serve drinks in tiny cups,
While hedgehogs join in, filling up.
Violet jokes tumble in the cool air,
While cats ponder why flowers care.

With each tick of the time, magic unfolds,
Even thorns join in, with stories bold.
Step down this path, where fun does ignite,
In a world of flowers, everything's bright!

## The Unfolding of Magical Flora

In a garden with blooms so round,
Wiggly worms dance on the ground.
Petals giggle with every breeze,
As bees get stuck in sticky cheese.

Butterflies in tutus prance,
While crickets play a silly dance.
The flowers chant in cheerful tones,
As squirrels steal their seeds and bones.

With every bloom, a joke unfolds,
The color wheel's full of bolds.
A daisy tells a pun or two,
While tulips laugh at what they knew.

So come and see this vibrant show,
Where nature's humor starts to flow.
In a swirl of petals and cheer,
Even grumpy toads find good beer!

## **A Tapestry of Petals and Promises**

On a canvas where colors collide,
A chamomile spills its secrets with pride.
Pansies mumble their gossip spree,
While roses yawn in a lazy glee.

A trumpet vine hoots a goofy tune,
As dandelion seeds float like a balloon.
Marigolds giggle at squirrels who steal,
While daisies whisper, "This is unreal!"

Promises woven in floral threads,
As the pollen parade dances on heads.
Letters of laughter sent on the breeze,
A confetti of joy that's sure to please.

So join this bloom-bopping merry band,
With petals aplenty in nature's hand.
A tapestry spun with a giggle or two,
Where every hue tells a joke just for you!

## Dreaming in Fragranced Hues

In a field where colors dream wide,
Lavenders puff with scents that glide.
Poppy petals peek with a grin,
While clovers play hide and seek within.

The nightingale croons a silly song,
As lilacs sway, feeling so strong.
Jasmine whispers sweet, cheeky rhymes,
And sunflowers strut, styling with lines.

Colors clash in a playful jest,
Each bloom dressed in a floral vest.
A riot of hues, a visual spree,
Dreaming of laughter, wild and free.

Join the escapade of nature's delight,
With fragrant whispers that tickle the night.
In this dreamland where flowers bloom wide,
Come share a giggle, come play on the side!

## Blossoms at the Edge of Time

At twilight's door, the petals sway,
A dance of silliness leads the way.
Wisteria winks with majestic flair,
While bumblebees giggle without a care.

Each bloom a story, a tale to share,
Where daisies declaim with flair.
The clock ticks backward in petal's play,
As night's perfume teases the day.

A daffodil jokes it's a 'cheery chap',
And nightshade sprawls in a cozy nap.
Time laughs aloud at the whimsy grown,
As flowers tell jokes to thrones of stone.

So step into this curious hour,
Where blossoms form a laughter tower.
In this garden where time blurs and bends,
Every petal whispers, "Come, make friends!"

## **Veils of Blooming Serenity**

In a garden where silence sways,
The flowers dance on sunny days.
A squirrel steals a flowered hat,
Wearing it like a dapper brat.

The bees buzz with a gossip's thrill,
As they sip nectar, a sweetened spill.
A hidden owl hoots, quite a tease,
Making rabbits laugh and wheeze.

Petals flurry in gentle swirls,
Playing tag like mischievous girls.
Underneath the blooming show,
A worm winks, putting on a show.

Nature's humor, fresh and light,
A symphony of silly sights.
With laughter sewn in every seam,
It's a funny flower-filled dream.

## Serenade of Fluffy Petals

In a field of fluffy cheer,
The flowers giggle, oh so dear.
One petals whispers, 'Over here!'
While a butterfly steals the beer.

A rabbit hops, with style and grace,
Bumping into a cactus face.
"Oops!" he gasps, with floppy ears,
Then mumbles jokes to cover fears.

The sun winks down, if you please,
While flowers giggle in the breeze.
A bumblebee sings off-key,
Hoping to get a deal on free.

So let's dance and twirl around,
In this whimsical, laughing ground.
Among the blooms, the jesters dwell,
In nature's jokes, we all excel.

## Luminous Blooms in the Evening Mist

By twilight's charm, the blooms ignite,
With glowing giggles, oh what a sight!
A raccoon joins with a graceful leap,
Stealing snacks, then back to sleep.

Under moonlight, a flower sways,
Telling tales of stick-your-tongue-out days.
A hedgehog chuckles, 'What a lark!'
As owls hoot from the nearest park.

The mint leaves plot a fragrant steal,
While fireflies dance with zest and zeal.
A lazy sloth claims the best view,
Says, 'I'll laugh at you from here, it's true!'

In this night of spark and fun,
Watch as nature's mischief runs.
Each bloom beams in playful mist,
Making magic no one can resist.

## Heartbeats Among Blossoming Trees

Beneath the trees, a playful tease,
A squirrel juggles acorns with ease.
He trips and falls, a comic break,
Leaves rustle, laughing for goodness' sake.

Fragrant whispers float on by,
As flowers wink and frogs all sigh.
A parade of ants march in rows,
While a blooming tulip strikes a pose.

Petals pirouette in air,
A butterfly shouts, 'Dare! I dare!'
The breeze joins in with a gentle push,
Spreading jokes in a playful hush.

Life's heartbeat thrums under the bloom,
In a world where laughter finds room.
So dance with me, let spirits soar,
In this garden of giggles galore!

## A Symphony of Color and Scent

Petals dance on breezy tunes,
Colors clash like silly cartoons.
A fragrance tickles, gives a grin,
While bees buzz by with little spin.

Lemon yellows, candy-pink,
In the garden, flowers wink.
One's too tall, the other shy,
Joking clouds just float on by.

A serenade of blooms in cheer,
They spread their joy from ear to ear.
A sneaky squirrel steals a snack,
While daisies giggle at his back.

What a show, this colorful spree,
Where petals whisper, "Come and see!"
With every rustle, laughter grows,
In nature's circus, delight flows.

## **Petals Adrift on Memory's Stream**

Floating thoughts like petals glide,
On a stream where dreams reside.
A ladybug joins the parade,
Wearing spots like a charade.

Old memories twirl in morning light,
Like socks that ended up in flight.
They laugh and play like kids at school,
In a splash of colors, oh so cool!

Each flower holds a story grand,
Of wind-tossed troubles, hand in hand.
A dragonfly tries to take a bow,
But slips and falls; it's just a wow!

Petals scatter, hearts will beam,
Floating softly on memory's stream.
Nothing's serious, all in jest,
Nature's humor, truly the best!

## Secrets Unraveled in Softest Hues

Amidst the garden's whispered tales,
A secret giggles while it sails.
Softest hues play peek-a-boo,
With all the petals, pink and blue.

A laugh erupts from blooms so bright,
As hidden critters spark delight.
The first to bloom won't take a nap,
While others plot their vibrant clap.

"Who's the prettiest?" the blooms debate,
While hummingbirds just can't wait.
They flit about like tiny jesters,
In pollen-fueled, buzzing festers.

Secrets twinkle in the air,
With blushing petals everywhere.
A butterfly winks, "It's all a show!"
As laughter spreads, they steal the glow.

## The Allure of Dawn's First Bloom

At dawn, the petals stretch and yaw,
With sleepy faces, nature's spa.
Bud, bud, bloom—the morning cheer,
"Do we smell fresh?" "Oh dear, oh dear!"

A sunflower flashes morning tea,
While others giggle in jubilee.
Forget-me-nots with tiny grins,
Remind the daisies of old wins.

The sunlight tickles every hue,
As blooms bloom faster than they knew.
"Who woke us up?" the roses pout,
As bees come buzzing all about.

Yet through the mirth, a lesson plagues,
That life's a show, so join the jags.
In every bloom, the morning's voice,
Calls us to laugh, to love, rejoice!

## **Petals in the Moonlight**

In twilight's glow, the blossoms sway,
Dancing shadows, come out to play.
A squirrel slips on petals bright,
As giggles spill into the night.

Fireflies wink, their lanterns flick,
A love-struck frog learns a new trick.
With each hop, it spins around,
A waltz of laughter, all abound.

The breeze brings whispers, crisp and sweet,
A raccoon taps his tiny feet.
He's got the moves, oh what a sight,
Groovin' under the starry light.

So come, let's join the commotion,
In this garden of sheer devotion.
With every step, let joy ignite,
As petals twirl in the moonlight.

## Woven Dreams of Pink and White

Petals play dress-up, pink and white,
Gossiping blooms, a lively sight.
The bees wear glasses, looking grand,
As they gossip with the flowers' band.

A baker ant brings treats so sweet,
Cheering up the blooms, quite the feat.
With icing made from pollen dust,
They dive right in, it's truly a must!

A butterfly floats, with flair it flies,
But crashes softly, oh what a surprise!
The flowers laugh, "Oh what a show,
Get back up, and give it a go!"

In this patch of dreams, all's quite clear,
Joy's woven tight, with chuckles near.
So let's sip nectar, share delight,
In this garden of pink and white.

## The Aroma of Dusk

In evening's hue, aromas swirl,
A perfume mix, a floral twirl.
Bees snore loudly, tired from work,
While ladybugs strut with a smirk.

Clouds parade in shades of rose,
While crickets strum with tiny toes.
Each whiff could make a lion laugh,
With silliness on a floral path.

As dusk deepens, the blooms conspire,
To make a cocktail of sweet desire.
A breeze carries tales from the past,
Of silly blooms, a comic blast!

So inhale deep, let joy abound,
In this fragrant realm of giggles found.
Where every scent is pure delight,
In the aroma of the dusk tonight.

## **Blossoms of a Timeless Tale**

In a garden steeped in lore and cheer,
Flowers weave stories for all to hear.
Each petal whispers a fun-filled rhyme,
Of antics alive, transcending time.

A jester bee with a tiny hat,
Juggles sweet pollen, what of that?
The daisies chuckle, oh what a game,
While tulips cheer him on by name.

With the sun setting, hues blend and glow,
A chorus of blooms in a vibrant show.
They bounce and sway, their laughter free,
In this timeless tale of harmony.

So take a seat, grab a cup of tea,
Join the laughter from a bloom or three.
In the saga of petals, fun won't fail,
As we delight in this timeless tale.

## Ethereal Blooms at Dusk

In twilight's glow, the flowers smirk,
Their petals jive, they like to lirk.
Bumblebees dance, with tiny feet,
As ants in tuxedos take a seat.

The shadows stretch with a giggle,
While frogs join in with a little wriggle.
The moon winks down with a candy grin,
As daisies whisper their cheeky sin.

Each blossom wears a silly hat,
Pansies prance like a jovial cat.
The evening breeze bursts into song,
While tulips tease—"You dance wrong!"

In the garden's fun, who needs a fuss?
Petunias shout, "Come join the bus!"
Let's revel in the blooms we see,
Where laughter blooms so naturally.

**Rain-kissed Petals and Sunlit Hues**

Rain-drops giggle on petals bright,
Tickling leaves in pure delight.
The sun pops out, a big ol' grin,
While flowers beckon, "Come and spin!"

With colors splashed like toddler art,
Each bloom declares, "I'm off the chart!"
Butterflies prance in a tight ballet,
As daisies say, "Not today, sorbet!"

The wind carries scents that tease and play,
Petal gossip from yesterday.
"Did you see how the lilacs swayed?"
"And the wildflowers? They never paid!"

In this wacky, flowery spree,
Each plant seems a host of glee.
Through sunlit hues and raindrop cheers,
They blossom loud, ignoring fears.

## In the Glow of Floral Reverie

Beneath the stars, the blossoms sway,
A fragrant crowd in their bouquet.
Roses chuckle at their own flair,
While tulips argue about their hair.

The moonlit dance floor starts to thump,
Petals bounce, and the stalks go jump.
A weedy bard recites some rhymes,
As other plants giggle at his crimes.

With all the colors in the night,
Every flower's a silly sight.
Pixies twirl like tops in flight,
While mossy rocks drift off, in spite.

In dreamy hues, the night's alive,
With floral pranks that twist and jive.
Join the laughter, soak in the view,
Nature's party is waiting for you!

## The Harmony of Blossom and Breeze

The breeze brings tunes to the flower crowd,
Each blossom nods, feeling quite proud.
Chirpy crickets hold a concert here,
While daffodils start to cheer!

The roses share their sweetest lore,
About the gardener's clumsy chore.
"Did you see him trip on the lawn?"
"Yeah, we bloomed extra bright at dawn!"

Petunia's wearing oversized shades,
As dandelions try to make some trades.
"Would you like some of my fluff?" they say,
While violets giggle and shout, "Hooray!"

In the garden's light, the fun won't cease,
Where every plant enjoys their peace.
With breezy songs and silly jives,
The blooms unite, oh how they thrive!

## Shadows of the Flowering Canopy

Beneath the blooms, the shadows play,
Where squirrels dance, they steal the day.
A wiggle here, a jump over there,
Nature's clowns without a care.

Bees wearing hats, they buzz in flight,
Chasing friends till the fall of night.
A flower sneezes, petals fly,
Who knew nature could be so spry?

Each moment wrapped in laughter's quilt,
While blossoms boast of their fine wilt.
The fragrance tickles noses, oh!
Who knew blossoms could steal the show?

In this shady world of blooming sights,
We giggle with the bugs in their flights.
Every leaf a joker in the breeze,
Rustling secrets with such ease.

## A Tapestry of Nature's Artistry

A canvas broad, with colors bright,
The flowers giggle in pure delight.
Petals whisper jokes, oh so sly,
While butterflies wink as they flutter by.

The daisies sport their polka dots,
While tulips brag of sunny spots.
A daffodil slips in the mud,
Laughing hard, it's all a flood!

Squirrels play cards under the sun,
Challenging birds to break and run.
With every bloom, more fun unfolds,
Nature's antics, worth their weight in gold.

Crickets chirp a rhythm sweet,
While blossoms bob to the playful beat.
What a show, with laughter entwined,
Nature's art, so whimsically designed.

## **Reveries in Soft Starlit Hues**

Under the moon, the blossoms glow,
As fireflies put on quite a show.
Petals hum tunes of night-time glee,
While the stars chuckle, can you see?

Crickets fashion tiny guitars,
Serenading dreams from afar.
A midnight bloom spills its tea,
All the flowers gossip, oh so free!

The nightingale sings a silly song,
While night-blooming jests dance along.
With laughter weaving through the dew,
Nature chuckles, who knew?

A breeze stirs giggles in darkened leaves,
As sleepy petals find their thieves.
Under this dome of serene light,
The flowers chuckle into the night.

## **Petal-Bound Dreams**

In a land where blooms all conspire,
Petal-bound dreams lift us higher.
A flower wishes for a new hat,
While bumblebees wear shoes that chat.

Ladybugs dance with tiny grace,
Playing tag in a floral race.
A tulip tells a corny pun,
Making all the daisies run.

Butterflies twirl in their silky coats,
Chasing rainbows in leaky boats.
With laughter stitched in every petal,
Nature's quirks, a joyous riddle.

As dreams take flight on breezy wings,
The world of blooms gives joy it brings.
With every tickle, every gleam,
Petal-bound laughter fuels the dream.

## Fragrant Secrets in the Dark

In the garden, whispers play,
Fragrant secrets drift away.
Squirrels giggle, kiss and tease,
Hiding snacks among the trees.

Moonlight dances, shadows prance,
Crickets join the midnight dance.
Who knew flowers felt so bold?
Their giggles soft, but tales are told.

Sneaky ants parade with pride,
Marching on, they won't subside.
Dancing petals, oh so bright,
Chasing dreams into the night.

Laughter bubbles, night's delight,
Floral dreams take wondrous flight.
If you listen, you will find,
Nature's jesters, so entwined.

## **Petals Floating on a Dream**

Petals float like fluffy pillows,
On a breeze, the laughter billows.
Bees in bowties, buzzing fast,
Join the party, what a blast!

Sunshine tickles every bloom,
Nature's chuckles fill the room.
Butterflies in shades of glee,
Dance along, so wild and free.

Raindrops drop in rhythmic beat,
Tiny tap dance on my feet.
Jumping puddles, splashes fly,
Clouds may grumble, but we'll try!

Floating dreams on petals' breeze,
A giggle here, a dance with ease.
Frogs in tuxedos croak a tune,
To the chorus of the moon.

## **Luminosity of the Southern Breeze**

The breeze sweeps in with feathered flair,
Whispers sing and twirl in air.
Sun-kissed petals start to sway,
An orchestra of blooms at play.

Fireflies wear their tiny hats,
Twinkling secrets, fancy chats.
Laughter holds a fragrant note,
Captured dreams in flowers' coat.

A dog named Gus joins with a bark,
Prancing through the glowing park.
He thinks he's part of this bouquet,
Plays tag with shadows, chases play.

Southern nights are full of cheer,
Lightning bugs, and friends draw near.
Every scent and laugh enchants,
Nature's ballet in moonlit pants.

# **Welcoming the Softness of Night**

Cuddly clouds creep, oh so sly,
Hugging stars as they pass by.
Nighttime cuddles, giggles thrum,
Catch a sweet scent, what's that yum?

Bumblebees in pajamas zoom,
Seeking snacks beneath the moon.
Chasing shadows, they convene,
Whisking by in buzzing teen!

With petals as soft as fluffy sheep,
Whispers tangled, secrets deep.
The moonlight winks, a cheeky gleam,
In this garden, dare to dream.

In this night, the silliness grows,
As flower jokes become the shows.
A blanket of laughter, twinkling bright,
Welcoming all to this wild night.

## Tales of the Blossoming Heart

In the garden, blooms so bright,
A squirrel dances, what a sight!
He thinks he's suave, with nuts in tow,
A real Casanova, putting on a show.

When petals fall, he does a spin,
A flower crown, he wears with grin.
Bee whispers sweet, they call him "King,"
He nods and struts, just doing his thing.

A ladybug joins, wears shades of red,
They groove together, no signs of dread.
With laughter ringing, the sun smiles wide,
In this floral kingdom, they take great pride.

The roses giggle, the daisies cheer,
As our squirrel prince spreads joy and cheer.
In this tale of blooms, with antics so smart,
Who knew nature held a funny heart?

## Fragments of a Dreaming Flower

A daisy dreamed of being a star,
It thought, 'Oh my! I've come so far!'
It donned a cape, made of green leaves,
A hero in bloom, that everyone believes.

A dandelion popped in, full of sass,
Said, 'You'll never pass, hey, look at the grass!'
But the daisy winked and whispered a line,
'I'm off to the moon, how about a sign?'

The wind chuckled loud, swirling all around,
As petals danced, above the ground.
"I'll be a star, just wait and see!"
The garden held its breath, laughing with glee.

Yet as the sun set, dreamers retreat,
The daisy just sighed, "I'll stick to my seat."
But who needs the stars when you've got this show?
In the world of dreams, the fun's never low!

## **Elysian Fields of Floral Delight**

In fields of petals, laughter rings,
Butterflies giggle, they flap their wings.
A sunbeam skips, so merry and bright,
Painting the flowers, a comical sight.

The tulips tease, with a playful sway,
'Who wore it better? Should we play?'
They dress in aprons, cooking up glee,
"Today's special? Pancakes, come see!"

The violets chuckle, rolling in clumps,
Joining a dance, amid the flower lumps.
A cactus popped up, wearing a frown,
"Do you need help? Or just want a crown?"

With laughter exploding, a whimsical spree,
"Come join the fun, in this floral decree!"
For in these fields, where joy takes flight,
Every petal's a giggle, an outright delight!

## The Enchantment of Floral Dreams

In a field of whimsy, blooms all around,
Petals are singing, a vibrant sound.
A sunflower bows, with a graceful nod,
"I'm the queen here, just give me a prod!"

A crooked rose chimed, "Not so fast, dear!"
"Your height's amusing, I've no need to fear!"
The tulips giggled, giving a cheer,
A flowery showdown, we've all gathered near.

With thorns in the mix, a prickly affair,
Yet all could laugh, no room for despair.
"Who will win?" echoed across the breeze,
As daisies whispered, "May the best one tease!"

But in this charm, where fun's the true prize,
Every leafy bicker brought smiles, not cries.
So here's to the blooms that keep spirits high,
In the world of flowers, we all fly sky-high!

## A Symphony of Fragrance

In gardens where the sweet scents play,
Petals dance in the sun's warm ray.
The bees buzz on their daily quest,
While squirrels wear nutty hats, quite dressed.

A breeze whispers secrets to the trees,
Who chuckle and sway with elegant ease.
Each bloom giggles at the passing bee,
As if to say, 'Come, laugh with me!'

The sky wears a hue of pastel delight,
And flowers perform in the soft twilight.
A waltz of colors in playful delight,
Forget the worries, it's a charming sight!

So let's raise a glass to this floral cheer,
Where silliness reigns, let's all draw near.
With laughter, we'll sip on nature's brew,
And dance 'neath the stars, just me and you.

## The Unfurling of Twilight

As twilight unfurls its golden thread,
The garden awakens from its floral bed.
With glee, the petals spread in their grace,
While crickets tune up their night-time bass.

A firefly flirts, its glow like a wink,
While shadows and blooms share a drink.
This merry mix of nature's delight,
In a cozy corner, fun takes flight.

The moon chuckles from its cozy throne,
Watching the leaves shake, all on their own.
Even the stars seem to giggle and tease,
As the night unfolds, it aims to please.

So let's toast to blooms and twinkling skies,
And laugh at the whispers of playful lies.
For in this realm where flowers dwell,
Life's simple magic casts a funny spell.

## Gentle Spirits of the Orchard

In orchards where the laughter echoes bright,
Fruit trees gossip under the moonlight.
With branches that sway like arms in play,
They share their secrets in a silly way.

Squirrels scurry about with charm,
Telling tales of mischief, causing alarm.
"Watch out for the pie!" one cheekily shouts,
While everyone else breaks into snickers and clouts.

The apples roll, a merry parade,
While pumpkins chuckle, their silly charade.
Each blossom sings tunes of life's blooper,
As laughter ignites like a sweet little trooper.

The spirits of the orchard, fun-loving and spry,
Invite us to join in, so let out a sigh.
This playful haven, with stories to tell,
Is a bright, cozy corner where joy fits so well.

## **Moonlit Tales of Resilience**

Under the moon's cheeky glow we stand,
With trees that dance to a whimsical band.
The stars twinkle proudly, their outfits aglow,
As the night unfolds tales of those who grow.

Sprouts of hope in each corner thrive,
Chasing the shadows, they feel so alive.
With roots that dig deep, like secrets they hold,
Every bloom whispers stories bold.

Laughter echoes through leafy halls,
As critters embark on their nightly calls.
The playful breeze pokes through the air,
It tickles the blossoms, without a care.

So here's to the night, with its jesters and thrills,
Resilience blooms, like daffodils on hills.
Let's toast to the magic, the fun, and the cheer,
For in this moonlit garden, laughter draws near!

## **Starlit Serenade in Bloom**

In the garden where giggles roam,
Flowers dance, and bees hum home.
A nightingale croons, off-tune delight,
While fireflies flash in a silly flight.

Petals in pajamas, having a blast,
Sharing secrets from the very last.
Laughter erupts as dew drops gleam,
Nature's jesters in a whimsical dream.

Silly shadows take a twirl,
Waltzing with ferns that softly twirl.
The moon chuckles, a silver grin,
As tulips giggle, letting fun in.

In this wacky world of floral cheer,
Every bud whispers, "Stay right here!"
A starlit serenade, oh what a sight,
Where laughter blooms and hearts take flight.

## **Garden of Whispered Wishes**

In the garden where wishes collide,
Daisies argue, petals aside.
Sunflowers gossip about the sun,
While daisies chant, "We're here for fun!"

Ladybugs share tales of their flight,
Frogs croak songs, oh what a sight!
With ticklish grass beneath our toes,
Laughter frolics where the wild thyme grows.

A breeze tickles with playful intent,
As blooms and bees have fun, in the scent.
Wishes murmur, "Make it come true,"
While sneaky snails play peek-a-boo!

In the corner, a gnome with a grin,
Hopes for a dance, let the fun begin!
In this garden of whispered wishes bright,
What a joy it is, this magical night.

## The Poetry of Sweet Surrender

A butterfly flutters, a laugh in flight,
Moths tickle blooms, what a silly sight!
The bumblebees buzz with gossip galore,
As blossoms open, shout, "We want more!"

With petals that twirl in a light-hearted chase,
And daisies that play a game of embrace.
The breeze tosses leaves with cheeky delight,
As vines begin dancing, oh what a night.

A whimsical waltz on a moonbeam's glow,
Where flowers are poets, just letting it flow.
In the garden where fun takes its throne,
Is a blossoming saga of sweetness grown.

So surrender to laughter, let joy take its flight,
In this playful parade of enchanting night.
A poem unfurls with each petal's song,
With laughter in bloom, where we all belong.

## Embracing the Essence of Spring

In the field where sunflowers chat,
They argue who's tallest, imagine that!
Dandelions giggle, puffing with pride,
As petals toss jokes in the sunlight's ride.

Tulips in tutus, dancing in line,
Forget-me-nots mutter, "Aren't we divine?"
A chorus of robins sings loudly and clear,
While the trees tap dance, oh so near.

Buds burst with laughter, colors anew,
As squirrels play tag, the whole day through.
Spring's essence a stage, a comedy show,
Where every bloom's part of the fun we sow.

So we embrace this season so grand,
Where whimsy and joy go hand in hand.
In this playful arena where flowers will sing,
Let's frolic in laughter, in the heart of Spring.

## Whispers of the Southern Blooms

In the garden, blooms take flight,
Chasing bees from morn till night.
Petals giggle in the breeze,
Tickling squirrels perched on trees.

A flower's blush, a sight to see,
As it winks at the honey bee.
"Hey there, buzz, don't steal my show!"
"Oh, darling blooms, we're all in the flow!"

Underneath the starry skies,
Raccoons dance with sweet surprise.
"Is that a bouquet, or a hat for me?"
"Let's wear these blooms, so fancy and free!"

Whispers fly from petal to petal,
As frogs croak gossip in the kettle.
"Did you see her in that new shade?"
"Oh honey, she simply must have paid!"

## Beneath the Velvet Petals

Softly falling, petals sway,
Beneath the blooms, we laugh and play.
A squirrel stole my sandwich, oh dear!
But those flowers keep me full of cheer.

The bees hold court, with buzzing rules,
While lizards bask, acting like fools.
"Who wore it best?" the daisies demand,
"I think I'm the fairest in the land!"

Frogs recite poetry, frogs with flair,
As crickets giggle, twirling in air.
"Ribbit, my friend, what's your favorite hue?"
"Oh, the one that matches my shoes, too!"

Sunshine dances on each blush,
A butterfly flits, causing a hush.
"Is that a cocktail or just lemonade?"
"Well, darling blooms, let's call it a trade!"

## Enchanted by Southern Grace

In a haze of jasmine and delight,
The daisies prance under moonlight.
"Did you hear my joke about the bee?"
"It buzzed right past me, can't you see?"

Hydrangeas whisper secrets sweet,
While sleepy owls tap their feet.
"Why do flowers never play cards?"
"Because they're afraid of getting charred!"

Butterflies flaunt their fancy flair,
As bumblebees gossip without a care.
"Have you seen the blooms in that roundabout?"
"Why yes, they just kicked beauty out!"

Evening falls with a playful tease,
In the garden, life's a breeze.
"Let's throw a party; the crickets agree!"
"When and where? I'll bring the brie!"

## The Secret Blooming Hour

Shadows play among the flowers,
As critters scheme for these secret hours.
"Is it cake or just a sweet illusion?"
"Oh, darling friend, it's a floral fusion!"

At twilight, blooms put on a show,
With laughter bubbling, stealing the glow.
The trees gossip with leaves aflutter,
"Who wore that shade? Was it butter?"

Twirling petals dance through the night,
While the moon grins with pure delight.
"Hey beetle, do you think it's fair?
You've got more legs, but I've got flair!"

As stars peek through, the blooms unite,
In a world of chuckles, everything's right.
"Who needs the sun when we have this?"
"Darling, just a flower, finding bliss!"

## The Poetry of Nature's Palette

In a garden where colors chat,
The roses wear hats, imagine that!
Lilies are gossiping about the breeze,
While daisies throw parties with utmost ease.

A paintbrush spills over the scene,
Tulips wear shoes, all shiny and clean.
Sunflowers dance, oh what a sight!
Swaying like dancers beneath starlit night.

Bees buzzing tunes in key of delight,
While butterflies play hide and seek just right.
Nature's palette, a whimsically wild spree,
Colors laughing joyfully, just like me.

So gather your crayons, let's make a mess,
With giggles and splashes, I must confess.
In this happy garden, chaos is bound,
In the poetry of nature, laughter is found.

## A Dance of Petals and Moonlight

Underneath a glowing moon's embrace,
Petals twirl in a playful race.
They shimmy and shake with the softest flair,
Sprinkling joy like confetti in the air.

The night blooms giggle with fragrant delight,
Dancing with shadows, oh what a sight!
Owl in a top hat, keen to join in,
As frogs play the drums with a happy grin.

Laughter echoes through the trees,
While crickets play symphonies with ease.
Fireflies flash a sparkly cue,
Telling all petals, "Come join the shoe!"

In this revelry under starlit beams,
Nature's humor spills over in dreams.
A night of fun, with petals in flight,
A dance that feels just so right.

## Secrets of the Blossomed Souls

Whispers of blooms hang in the air,
Secrets shared without a care.
Petals giggle, oh what a sound,
Telling tales where joy is found.

The tulip's gossip might make you grin,
As they tease the snails about their spin.
Breezes carry laughter, jazzing about,
While busy bees hum, hopping about.

Dandelions plot their fluffy delight,
Blowing wishes away into the night.
In this flowered world, you'll soon see,
The secrets bloom like a wild jubilee.

With every petal, a giggle, a jest,
Nature's whispering, truly the best.
Join the fun and forget the woes,
In the garden where laughter freely flows.

## **Petal-Soft Dreams of the Night Sky**

In moonlit dreams, petals drift and sway,
Soft as whispers in the night's play.
They ride on breezes, floating so free,
Making wishes while dancing with glee.

Clouds wear disguises, playful and bright,
As petals steal glances, what a funny sight!
Stars twinkle brightly, like winking friends,
In this comedy where nature transcends.

While owls tell jokes beneath the moonbeam,
A chorus of flowers joins in the theme.
Petals giggle and spread silly cheer,
Creating a tapestry of dreams we hold dear.

So let's drift away and dance with delight,
In this petal-soft world, everything feels right.
With each tiny laugh, the night sings along,
In dreams spun of petals, we all belong.

www.ingramcontent.com/pod-product-compliance
Lightning Source LLC
Chambersburg PA
CBHW070749220426
43209CB00083B/195